A

Literature Unit

for

Dragonwings

by Laurence Yep

Written by Mari Lu Robbins

Illustrated by Keith Vasconcelles

Teacher Created Materials, Inc.

P.O. Box 1040
Huntington Beach, CA 92647
©1993 Teacher Created Materials, Inc.
Made in U.S.A.

ISBN 1-55734-429-9

Table of Contents

Introduction

The young person who learns to love books early in life is lucky, indeed, because he or she will have friends for life. A good book informs us and inspires us. It fills our hours with pleasure, knowledge, and companionship, and it can fill our minds with dreams and help us set goals. *Dragonwings* is such a book, one to be treasured throughout youth and on into adulthood.

In *Literature Units*, we have taken great care to choose books that will be treasured.

In this literature unit, teachers will find the following features to aid and supplement their own individual techniques.

- Sample Lesson Plans

- Pre-reading Activities

- A Biographical Sketch of the Author

- A Book Summary

- Vocabulary Lists and Suggested Vocabulary Ideas

- Chapters grouped for study with each section including a(n):
    - *quiz*
    - *hands-on project*
    - *cooperative learning activity*
    - *cross-curricular connection*
    - *extension into the reader's life*

- Post-reading Activities

- Book Report Ideas

- Research Ideas

- A Culminating Activity

- Three Different Options for Unit Tests

- A Bibliography

- An Answer Key

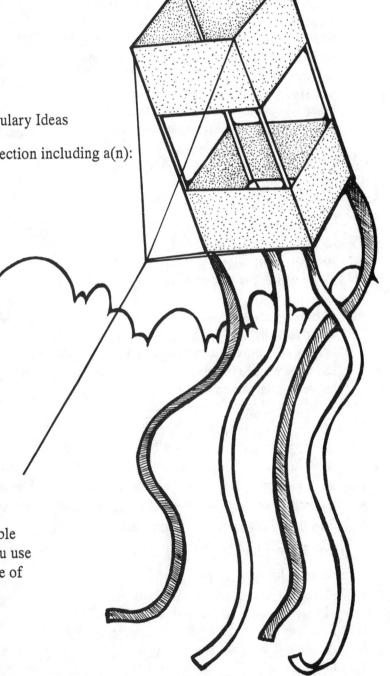

We are confident that this unit will be a valuable addition to your planning, and hope that as you use our ideas, your students will increase the circle of "friends" they have in books!

Sample Lesson Plans

Each of the lessons suggested below can take from one to several days to complete.

Lesson 1

- Introduce and complete some or all of the pre-reading activities found on page 5.
- Read "About the Author" with your students. (page 6)
- Introduce the vocabulary list for Section 1. (page 8)

Lesson 2

- Work in cooperative groups to complete the Anticipation Guide. (page 13)
- Read Chapters 1 and 2. As you read, discuss the vocabulary words as they are used in the context of the story.
- Choose a vocabulary activity. (page 9)
- Make Chinese lanterns. (pages 11-12)
- Read Tang poetry. Write simple four-line poems. (page 14)
- Begin Reading Response Journals. (page 15)
- Administer the Section 1 quiz. (page 10)
- Introduce the vocabulary list for Section 2. (page 8)

Lesson 3

- Read Chapters 3 through 5. As you read, discuss the vocabulary words as they are used in the story.
- Choose a vocabulary activity. (page 9)
- Learn to make a kite. (page 17)
- Play with Chinese tops. (page 18)
- Discuss the book in terms of the history of Chinese immigration to America. (page 19)
- Write graffiti messages. (page 20)
- Administer the Section 2 quiz .(page 16)
- Introduce the vocabulary list for Section 3. (page 8)

Lesson 4

- Read Chapters 6 through 8. As you read, discuss the words as they are used in the book.
- Choose a vocabulary activity. (page 9)
- Make gingerbread men. (page 22)
- Write "daffynitions." (page 23)
- Make 3-D glasses and discuss the book in terms of stereopticons and 3-D vision. (pages 24-25)
- Find proverbs to share with the class. (page 26)
- Administer the Section 3 quiz. (page 21)
- Introduce the vocabulary for Section 4. (page 8)

Lesson 5

- Read Chapters 9 and 10. Discuss the vocabulary words and their meanings in Section 4.
- Make a model seismograph. (page 28)
- Write and perform a Readers' Theater about events after the earthquake. (page 29)
- Discuss a model airplane in terms of measurement (Answer Key, page 48) and complete the related activities on page 30.
- Design a poster to find the owners of a kitten lost during the quake. (page 31)
- Administer the Section 4 quiz. (page 27)
- Introduce vocabulary list for Section 5. (page 8)

Lesson 6

- Read Chapters 11 and 12.
- Design a kite or a flying machine. (page 33)
- Search out aviation trivia. (page 34)
- Learn about airplanes. (pages 35-36)
- Write a letter to Moon Shadow's mother. (page 37)
- Administer Section 5 quiz. (page 32)

Lesson 7

- Discuss any questions your students may have about the story. (page 38)
- Assign book reports and research projects. (pages 39-40)
- Re-evaluate the Anticipation Guide and discuss changes of opinion. (page 13)
- Begin work on the culminating activity. (pages 41-42)

Lesson 8

- Administer Unit Tests 1, 2 and/or 3. (pages 43-45)
- Discuss the test answers and responses.
- Discuss the students' opinions and enjoyment of the book.
- Provide a list of related reading for the students. (page 46)

Lesson 9

- Celebrate the Chinese luncheon and kite festival. (pages 41-42)

Before the Book

Before reading *Dragonwings*, it will be very helpful to learn something about the time period and the cultural framework in which the book is set because the student's prior knowledge of the background of the story is crucial to that student's understanding of the book. It also will be beneficial to use some general pre-reading ideas to enable the students to better focus on the meaning of the literature. You might try some of these ideas in your class.

1. Predict what the story might be about by hearing the title.

2. Predict what the story might be about by looking at the cover.

3. Discuss other books by Laurence Yep that students may have read.

4. Discuss historical fiction.

5. As part of a bulletin board display on literature to be read during the current year, make a time line showing the relationship of the time period covered by *Dragonwings* (1903-1910) and other literature of the day to the present time period and today's literature.

6. Discuss the immigration history of the Chinese people into the United States. Ask the following questions:

    • Why did thousands of Chinese come here?

    • How were they treated when they got here?

    • What kinds of jobs did they take when they came?

    • How did they adapt their customs and traditions to life in America?

7. Discuss the history of aviation in America. Windrider, father of the narrator of *Dragonwings*, is a kite maker and is fascinated by flying. His dream is to build an aeroplane which will fly. How would his dream fit into what was happening at that time regarding flight?

8. Discuss the role of the family in Chinese culture. How are ancestors looked upon by the Chinese, and what part do they play in the life of the people?

9. Read about Angel Island, the island to which Moon Shadow of *Dragonwings* was sent when he first arrived in America. All of the early Chinese immigrants spent time on Angel Island when they came here.

10. Show a video of the land and people of China.

11. Individually or in groups, write a narration of how it might be to journey to a distant land, knowing you would live there among people who frighten you and whose ways are very different from your own. Write a brief answer to the question: What kind of person will take a risk, even though he or she is frightened?

About the Author

Laurence Yep was born in San Francisco on June 14, 1948. His early school experience was in a bilingual school in Chinatown, and he did not really encounter "white American culture" until his high school years. Because of this, his first literature interest was science fiction with its tales of aliens and strange new worlds.

Yep first wanted to be a chemist, but a teacher made him send some writing to a national magazine in order to get an "A" in her class, and his natural talent led him into professional writing soon after. He received a penny a word for his first short story.

After attending Marquette University, Yep received his Bachelor's Degree from the University of California, Santa Cruz, and his Ph.D from the State University of New York at Buffalo in 1975. He won the Book-of-the-Month Award writing fellowship in 1970. He now lives in California.

The teacher who first encouraged Yep to submit for publication started him on a very productive career. Laurence Yep's works include *Sweetwater, Child of the Owl, Kind Hearts and Gentle Monsters, Dragon of the Lost Sea, The Serpent's Children, Dragon Steel, Mountain Light,* and *The Rainbow People.*

Dragonwings is a Newbery Honor Book, and *Child of the Owl* is an American Library Association Notable Children's Book.

As Laurence Yep was researching his heritage for the background information of *Dragonwings*, he stumbled upon the story of Joe Guey, a Chinese man who, in 1909, flew an airplane he had built. The plane flew over the Oakland hills in California for 20 minutes. Laurence Yep decided to use the facts about the flight and to create a character for the story based on Joe Guey. The fictionalized aviator became Windrider, and the story is told by Young Moon Shadow, Windrider's son.

Six years of research for *Dragonwings* revealed that many Chinese who came to the United States in the early 1900's were men who, due to economic or legal factors, arrived without their families. These men became part of a "bachelor society" within the Chinese community. Eventually, members of this society sent for their sons or other male relatives to replace them when they grew old. Yep decided to incorporate these elements of his research into the story of *Dragonwings*.

Dragonwings

by Laurence Yep

(Harper & Row, 1975)

(Available in Canada, UK, and Australia from Harper Collins)

Until the letter arrived from America, saying it was time for him to join his father in the Land of the Golden Mountain, Moon Shadow had never left his small village in China, nor had he ever seen his father. Now he was sailing toward the fabled land where gold was to be had by all.

Life would not be easy in the new land. The people were strange; they spoke another language and followed customs much different from those he knew, and they sometimes could be dangerous. One never knew what to expect.

But what a man was this father he had never known! Moon Shadow quickly grew to love and respect this man who was so bright, virtuous, and courageous, and who dreamed of flying. Together they set about building a wonderful flying machine.

Dragonwings is an adventure set in the early twentieth century, a time of invention, of earthquake, and of fire. It also is a beautifully written poem in tribute to the Chinese who came to America and molded themselves to their new land in their own particularly unique way. For Moon Shadow, it is a time of growth as he learns to adapt to his new life until it no longer seems strange or frightening. For his father, Windrider, it is the land of golden opportunity where one can make one's dream come true.

Inspiring and original, *Dragonwings* describes early twentieth-century San Francisco, its Chinese-American community, and the cultural heritage it brought from the old country, the heroism and cowardice after the 1906 earthquake, and the creativity, intelligence, and daring of one man.

Vocabulary Lists

SECTION 1

lynch	Tang	heirloom	gnarled	unperturbed
immigrant	flatiron	vendor	superior	virtue
attired	translucent	incense	dynasty	phoenix
testimony	insolent	ornamentation	protrude	zinc
conventional	Buddhist	queue	casual	intention
dictation	soar	dowry	principle	elfin
amiable	prosperity	pious	despair	vibrate

SECTION 2

construct	filament	taint	diameter	mater
remnant	skirmish	poultice	iridescent	rheumatic
mournful	flourish	crystal set	sapphire	malicious
quaver	imperial	dwindle	mortal	dubious
malleable	livery	embodiment	dirigible	abacus
device	phenomenal	pun	specimen	residue
sinew	exuberance	meticulous	oppression	skeptical

SECTION 3

poultry	Victorian	methodical	loin cloth	gingham
antiquated	luminous	tentative	prime	wingspan
skeptical	amulet	tenement	turret	illusion
heathen	stereopticon	resonant	benevolent	vehement
schematics	jargon	lurid	parlor	celluloid
stark	customary	abstract	depict	repertory
propriety	sinuous	aeronautical	erratic	configuration

SECTION 4

passage	reckoning	persecute	ominous	debris
desolate	menacing	unruly	indignant	antique
venerable	cherish	monopolize	somber	choler
steeple	querulous	candelabrum	shanghaier	fermented
martial law	intact	vibration	taut	pagan
boycott	undulate	boisterous	suppress	moral
conscience	makeshift	fastidious	elaborate	sentimental

SECTION 5

plateau	helter-skelter	circumstance	restore	visible
pivot	christen	consecrate	plucky	perspective
abominable	lavish	ramshackle	writhe	revelation
strut	quicksilver	warp	spectator	shrewd
extension	accompany	penance	compensation	scavenger
handyman	varicolored	faze	mechanism	vertical
practical	contraption	sacred	tendril	whelped

Vocabulary Activity Ideas

This unit contains a vocabulary list for each section. There are many ways for the students to study the words, both individually and in groups. The words should be defined as they are used in *Dragonwings*, and then be used by the students in various ways to reinforce the meanings. The activities below give some ideas as to how the vocabulary words in *Dragonwings* may be studied.

❏ **Learn Words of the Day.** Have a given number of vocabulary words listed on the chalkboard for the first activity of the day. When the students come into the class, they go into pre-assigned groups. They divide up the words on the board among themselves and look up the meanings. The meanings are presented to the class, first orally, then written on the board. The class members copy the words and meanings into their reading journals or into vocabulary booklets. After the section has been read, the students discuss each word, then underline the correct meanings as the words have been used in *Dragonwings*. This is an excellent "sponge activity" to get the class going while attendance and other business is taken care of.

❏ **Put the words into crossword puzzles** or have the students make up crosswords with them to reinforce understanding of meanings.

❏ **Make word search puzzles** or have the students make them. Duplicate for the class, and have the students use fluorescent or neon markers to highlight the words when they find them. This helps to reinforce the students' sight vocabulary.

❏ **Play categories.** This is a good vocabulary activity to use with the whole class. As a group, sort the words into, for example, adjectives, nouns, and verbs. As each word is categorized, the reason for its being in that particular list is discussed, remembering that the words need to be used as they are used in *Dragonwings*. This provides an opportunity to talk about multiple meanings and how one often must know how a word is being used in context before one can know what that word means. One also needs to know how the word is being used in order to categorize the word.

❏ **Go fishing.** Vocabulary words are written on slips of paper and put into a container of some kind. Each student "fishes" one word from the container, looks it up, and reports back to the class as to the meaning(s) of the word. Students record the meanings in their reading journals or into vocabulary booklets.

❏ **Conduct a survey.** Each student is assigned one word from the list. The student then asks as many people as he can find at school and at home what the word means. If the person does not know, he or she makes a guess, and the student writes down whatever the person says. When the class comes back together the next day, they compare the "meanings" they were able to collect, then look up the words to find the actual meanings. This is a fun homework assignment.

Quiz Time

1. Who says, "There's nothing I can't do. I can dig up a mountain, drink up a lake, outrun the wind"?

   _____

2. What do the Chinese people call themselves? _____

   _____

3. Where are Hand Clap and Moon Shadow taken when they first arrive in San Francisco?

   _____

   _____

4. Why do the people of the Middle Kingdom call America the Land of the Golden Mountain?

   _____

   _____

   _____

5. How had Moon Shadow's grandfather died? _____

   _____

6. What is a demon? _____

   _____

7. How does the Lee family of men support itself in San Francisco? _____

   _____

8. Why are there very few Chinese women in San Francisco? _____

   _____

9. From whom does Uncle Bright Star claim to have taken his ideas of "the superior man?"

   _____

   _____

10. Describe the "silly toy" which Windrider gives to Moon Shadow when he arrives in San Francisco.

    _____

    _____

Chinese Lanterns

In Chinese schools, making "lanterns" out of egg shells has long been a favorite craft activity. It is easy and requires very few materials, but you will need to be very careful, because the materials are fragile. Use bright colors, especially red, yellow, and green.

Materials

- one raw, white egg
- two strips of colored paper, 1 inch (2.54 cm) by 4 ¼ inches (5.7 cm)
- one piece of paper, 1 ½ inches (3.8 cm) square
- one piece of fine wire 6 inches (15 cm) long
- one piece of fine wire 2 inches (5 cm) long
- two small wooden slivers from non-lighting end of a wooden match, or two pieces of broom straw, ³/₈ inch (1 cm) long
- watercolors and brush, or colored markers
- nail or seam ripper

Directions

1. With a nail or the point of a seam ripper, very carefully poke a small hole in each end of the egg. Enlarge the opening to no more than ¹/₁₀ inch (.25 cm). Blow out the liquid.

2. Wrap one end of each piece of wire around a wooden sliver, taking care not to overlap it, as overlapping will make the wire too thick.

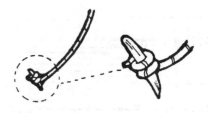

3. Insert the end of the 6-inch wire and sliver into the hole at the top of the egg. Insert the 2 inch wire with sliver into the bottom of the egg. You now have wires coming from each end of the egg.

4. Bend each piece of paper into a ring shape and glue the ends together, using as little glue as will hold the paper in shape. Allow the glue to dry.

Chinese Lanterns *(cont.)*

5. Using as little glue as will secure the paper to the egg, glue one paper ring to each end of the egg.

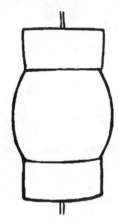

6. With paints or markers, paint or draw a design on the egg. Traditional designs include calligraphy, birds, fish, or flowers, but you may use any design you wish, even a flag or animal.

7. Cut ³/₄ inch (1.9 cm) slits along one edge of the square piece of paper to make fringe.

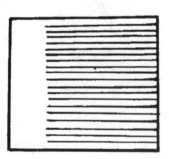

8. Wrap the entire length of the solid edge of fringe around the wire at the bottom of the egg to make a hanging trim.

9. Wrap the narrow strip of paper over the top of the fringed paper to finish it off.

    And there you have it—a miniature Chinese lantern to decorate your room or to hang as an ornament on a tree!

12

Anticipation Guide

The purpose of an anticipation guide is to increase comprehension of a story by having the students bring to mind situations with which they are familiar and which are similar in some ways to the situations in the story.

Before reading *Dragonwings,* show the book to the students and tell them that they will read this book.

In groups of three or four, have students fill out the anticipation guide. Emphasize to them that answers are opinions only and will not be graded. Collect when finished.

After anticipation guides are collected, discuss the answers with the entire class. The same questions will be given to the students after the book is completed, and any changes of opinion between the first and second times will be discussed.

Anticipation Guide

Write **agree** or **disagree** after each statement below.

1. Nobody is all bad or good.

   _____

2. Good people sometimes do bad things.

   _____

3. It is best to ignore someone who picks on you.

   _____

4. Disasters bring out the best in people.

   _____

5. Disasters bring out the worst in people.

   _____

6. America is the land of opportunity for anyone who wants to become successful.

   _____

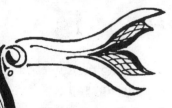 

Tang Poetry

Chinese poetry has been written for thousands of years. There are over 5,500 Chinese characters that are combined into words, and it would seem that just learning to read the language would take a lifetime. Yet most people in China have written in verse throughout the centuries. Writing poetry for the Chinese has been a natural and solacing part of life, seeing beauty in an imaginative phrase, as well as in nature.

The poems below were written during the Tang Dynasty (A.D. 618-907). Some of the greatest Chinese poets from that era include, Wang Wei, Li Bo, Du Fu, and Bo Juyi. Read the following very old Tang poems. Then discuss what you think the meaning of the poems might be and your observations about the style of the poems.

He Chih-Chang

賀知章

I left home young. I return old.
Speaking as then, but with hair grown thin;
And my children, meeting me, do not know me.
They smile and say: "Stranger, where do you come from?"

Li Yi

李益

Since I married the merchant of Ch'u-t'ang
He has failed each day to keep his word...
Had I thought how regular the tide is,
I might rather have chosen a river-boy.

A Song of Pure Happiness

下江陵

Her robe is a cloud, her face a flower;
Her balcony, glimmering with the bright spring dew,
Is either the tip of earth's Jade Mountain
Or a moon-edged roof of paradise.

Can you write a simple four-line poem like one of these? Remember to write about one thing or one person. Keep your language simple, yet draw a word picture with your poem.

Reading Response Journals

Reading response journals can be a very important addition to the reading of a book. They can help to personalize the story by relating it to real life and by helping show alternative ways of dealing with situations. This can be particularly significant when the book is a historical novel like *Dragonwings*, because young people do not always see themselves as a part of the flow of history. Without guidance, students may feel that people of the past seem too remote.

The reading response journal can be the conduit which relates past to present for the young reader.

To make the reading response journal most effective, use all or some of the following tips.

- ❑ Provide a purpose for the reading. Let your students know that what they are about to read is interesting and important to them.

- ❑ Before they do the reading, give the students the question they will be asked to answer in their journals. This will enable them to think about the answer in the course of the reading. Sample questions for each chapter in *Dragonwings* can be found on page 38.

- ❑ Before reading, give a preview of the main events which will be covered in a reading assignment, including any significant historical or geographical data which is relevant. Ask questions to determine whether the students know important background information.

- ❑ Use a variety of reading strategies, both oral and silent. Read to them as they listen or as they follow in the book. Allow them to read together or alone. Dramatize the reading with your voice and body language. Help them to see humor. Point out some of the literary devices the writer has used, so they will understand that a writer writes intentionally, not in a vacuum. Show your appreciation for the figurative language in the text.

- ❑ Allow students to copy final drafts of formal written papers into their journals. This will give them a chronological record of their writing and become a source of pride for them. If possible, store the journals in the classroom. They will stay neater and always be available.

- ❑ Reading response journals also may be used to record vocabulary words and definitions, as well as the definitions of literary terms.

- ❑ Allow students time to write. Five or ten minutes is usually sufficient.

Quiz Time

1. On the back of this paper, name three of the main events of this section.

2. Who causes many problems because of a bad habit? _____

3. What happens between Black Dog and Moon Shadow which will have a big effect on Moon Shadow and Windrider's lives?

   _____

   _____

4. Why does Windrider not send for Moon Shadow's mother?

   _____

   _____

5. Describe the encounter between Mr. Alger and Windrider and tell what the result of that encounter will be to Moon Shadow and Windrider.

   _____

   _____

6. Why does Windrider believe he was a dragon in a former life?

   _____

   _____

7. What is the importance to Windrider of having been a dragon?

   _____

   _____

8. When Windrider leaves the laundry, where will he go to work?

   _____

   _____

9. What skill does Windrider have which will enable him to live in the land of demons?

   _____

   _____

10. On the back side of this paper, tell how Windrider earns the friendship and loyalty of the Dragon King.

16

Go Fly a Kite!

Chinese boys and girls draw from their long kite-making history each year when many contests are held to determine who can make and fly the most beautiful kite. Kites may be shaped in the form of a dragon, a bird such as the swallow that Windrider made for Moon Shadow, or in any geometrical shape imaginable. They can be made by a group or an individual, and are often very elaborate.

Kites have been flown in the western world for centuries as well, some of them large enough to carry people! In fact, the Army and Navy of England used a train of kites to carry a man in the air so that he could see the enemy.

Kites can be made from a kit. However, you can make a basic diamond-shaped kite from a few simple materials you may already have or can easily find.

Materials: two wooden slats, or two pieces of bamboo (One piece should be about 3 feet/1 m; the other should measure about 1 ½ feet/.5 m.); carpenter's file; lightweight fabric enough to fit across the kite and for the tail ribbons; scissors; roll of cotton cord or all fiber twine; glue, or needle and thread; a winder on which to wind the twine (Paper towel tubes, pencils, or dowels work well.)

Directions

1. To make the frame of the kite, form a cross shape with the two sticks. Tie them together with cotton cord or twine.

2. Use a file to make notches in the ends of the sticks. Run string through notches.

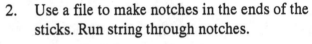
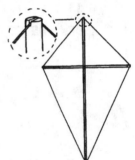

3. Lay the frame over the fabric. Cut the material using the frame pattern, allowing about 1 ½ inches (3-4 cm) of excess material all around. Fold the extra material over the cord or twine.

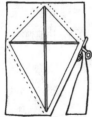

4. Glue or sew the fold to cover the cord or twine.

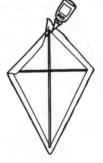

5. Make a bridle cord by tying a piece of cord or twine slightly longer than the longest stick to both ends of the long stick. Next, tie a very long piece of twine to the bridle cord. Make a fabric tail for the bottom of your kite to give it balance. Now you are ready to send your kite up, up, and away!

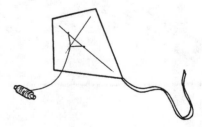

Chinese Tops

Chinese children play a centuries-old game with handmade tops. In this game, everyone wins except one. This is how the game is played.

Any number of people put their tops into a circle about 24 inches (61 cm) in diameter on the ground. A fine wire is tightly coiled around the neck of each top. One person at a time rapidly pulls the wire from his top, causing the top to spin. The object of the game is to get out of the circle. However, other tops are knocked out of the circle as well. The last person whose top is still left in the circle is the loser—sort of like being in "the mush pot."

Most Chinese children make their own tops from a round piece of wood. If you live near a Chinatown or a Chinese import store, you may be able to find plastic tops which are sometimes imported.

To make your own Chinese top, you will need a short, sharpened pencil with a grooved metal eraser top, a 1 ½" (3.8 cm) thread spool (wooden), a coping saw, tape, thin wire, and a pocket knife.

Directions:

1. Using a saw, cut the spool to a length of ³/₄" (1.8 cm). Be sure an adult supervises or does this activity.

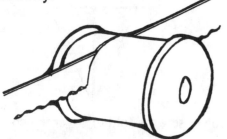

2. Push the pencil into the center hole of the spool. If it is loose, wrap tape around the pencil area that fits inside the spool.

3. If the pencil's diameter is too thick, whittle it down with a pocket knife until it fits.

4. Wrap a length of wire several times around the metal pencil top, so that when it is pulled, the homemade top will spin.

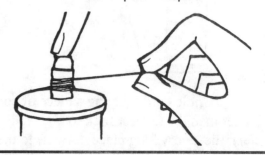

A Closer Look at Angel Island

Moon Shadow did not like to talk or think about it much, the two-story barracks where he and the other immigrants from China stayed for two weeks. Around the turn of the century, so many immigrants went through the barracks at Angel Island that it was often called the "Ellis Island of the West" after the famed island in New York harbor to which European immigrants were taken.

Angel Island, mountainous and covered with grass and forest, lies almost in the center of San Francisco Bay. Its human-inhabited history extends back at least two thousand years, first as home to the Miwok Indians, then by the Spaniards and Americans.

Angel Island still lies in San Francisco Bay, and the barracks in which Moon Shadow lived and slept for two weeks still stand. Long after Moon Shadow's stay there, Angel Island was used as a military induction center, then as a camp for Japanese prisoners of war during World War II. The island now is a state park of California and is visited by many thousands each year.

You may write **as a class** to the Angel Island Association to learn more about this small island with the fascinating history. The Angel Island Association is a non-profit organization whose mission is to share and care for Angel Island. You may visit the island and see the barracks where many Asian immigrants spent their first days and weeks in the United States. You may also wish to visit Camp Reynolds and Fort McDowell, which are also on the island.

The address of the association follows:

Angel Island Association
Angel Island State Park
P.O. Box 866
Tiburon, CA 94920
Tel: (415) 435-3522

Angel Island Graffiti

One of the most interesting things about the barracks on Angel Island is the graffiti on the wooden walls. Having no paper on which to write, and probably feeling very lonely and scared after a hard voyage followed by detention on a strange island, many of the early residents, and some of the later ones as well, wrote or carved messages on the walls. Poetry, entreaties, and commentaries were written, many of which are still visible.

Imagine that you are being held in the barracks on Angel Island. You have just completed a long, uncomfortable journey across the ocean. You have not committed a crime. You are being given strange foods to eat by people you believe to be demons. You are sleeping in a strange bed. You do not speak the language of the people in authority, but you read their body language; their facial expressions say that you are considered by them to be less than important. You do not know why you are here or how long you will have to stay. And you have no choice as to whether you stay or leave; some unknown person will decide that for you.

What kind of graffiti would you write? What would you want to say to someone who comes after you? What legacy would you leave?

On the back of the page, write some of the thoughts and emotions you would want to express on the walls so that those people coming after you could read them and appreciate your plight.

Quiz Time

1. On the back of this page, name three important events in this section.

2. Who does Moon Shadow call the "demoness"?

_____

_____

3. How do Windrider and Miss Whitlaw react when Moon Shadow gobbles down the cookies?

_____

_____

4. What opinion does Miss Whitlaw and Moon Shadow each have about dragons?

_____

_____

5. How does Moon Shadow solve the problem with Jack?

_____

_____

6. What does Robin use to teach Moon Shadow how to read the demon's writing?

_____

_____

7. To whom does Moon Shadow write a letter, and what response does he get?

_____

_____

8. Describe the picnic on which Moon Shadow and his father go with Robin and Miss Whitlaw.

_____

_____

9. How do Moon Shadow and Miss Whitlaw educate each other?

_____

_____

10. On the back of this page tell what Windrider wants to do more than anything and how he sets about doing it.

Gingerbread Men

When the Demoness, Miss Whitlaw, offered Moon Shadow some brown-colored things shaped like men with eyes, noses, and button coats made of icing, he was not about to trust her. He had already tasted the "awful, greasy" white stuff—milk—and he was certain these gingerbread cookies had to be even worse. Much to his surprise, however, they were wonderful, and having eaten one of them, he could not stop himself from eating more. You will like them, too, especially when you have made them yourself! Try this recipe on for size!

Ingredients

- ¹/₄ cup (60 mL) butter or margarine
- ¹/₂ cup (125 mL) white or brown sugar
- ¹/₂ cup (125 mL) dark molasses
- 3 ¹/₂ cups (.8 L) flour
- 1 teaspoon (5 mL) baking soda
- ¹/₄ teaspoon (about 1 mL) cloves
- ¹/₂ teaspoon (about 3 mL) cinnamon
- 1 teaspoon (5 mL) ginger
- ¹/₂ teaspoon (about 3 mL) salt

Directions

1. Heat oven to 350 degrees Fahrenheit (176 degrees Celsius).

2. Blend butter or margarine and white or brown sugar until creamy.

3. Beat in dark molasses. Set aside.

4. In a separate bowl, sift the flour. Then, resift the flour with the baking soda, cloves, cinnamon, ginger, and salt.

5. Add the sifted ingredients to butter mixture, alternating with 5 tablespoons (75 mL) water.

6. Finish mixing the dough with your hands.

7. To make gingerbread men, roll a ball for a head, a larger ball for the body, and cylinders for the arms and legs. Stick them together on a cookie sheet to form the gingerbread man shape. Bake for about 8 minutes or until done.

8. Make an icing paste of confectioner's sugar, food coloring, and a few drops water. Use icing to trim. Paint on trim for gingerbread men. That's all there is to it!

Daffynitions

It is very difficult to start a new life as Moon Shadow did, in another country whose language is totally different from yours. English and Chinese are very unlike each other in many respects. For example, in writing English, we use 26 letters which we combine in hundreds of thousands of ways to make words. When writing Chinese, each word is written by a separate "character" which in turn is given a certain sound depending on how it is being used. The meaning depends on how the word is sounded. It is small wonder that Moon Shadow had some confusing and frustrating times while he was learning to read and write English!

Even those of us who have grown up speaking English sometimes have trouble hearing or understanding our "mother tongue." Nevertheless, English is still a rich and versatile language, and it is sometimes possible to be creative and have a little fun with it at the same time.

Activity

One way to enjoy the English language is by thinking up daffy-definitions—that is, by writing definitions which sound as though they might really define the word in question. For example, read the following:

aftermath: the period following math (Of course!)

arithmetic: a subject that is hard work, because of all the numbers you have to carry

library: the tallest building in the world, because it has the most stories

mushroom: place where they store the school cafeteria food

yardstick: a creature that has three feet but can not walk

data: what a baby computer calls its father

Now it is your turn. In groups of three to five, write definitions (daffy-definitions) of the following words. Write a story in which you use as many as possible.

Word List

bookworm	debate
cafeteria	kindergarten
orange	smile
halo	conference
solar	adolescent

3-D Vision

The first time Moon Shadow saw Robin he was awed by something she had in her hand—"a long rod with lenses at one end and a card, with two pictures on it, held in a rack at the other." The object of Moon Shadow's fascination was a *stereopticon*.

What seemed like magic to Moon Shadow was, in fact, a simple device which uses the brain's ability to take two slightly different two-dimensional (width and length) images seen by the two eyes from slightly different angles and put them together to form one image which also seems to have depth.

Stereopticon

A person looks through the two eyepieces of the stereopticon at two pictures side-by-side. Each eye sees one picture.

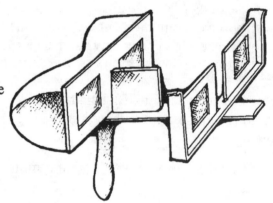

The brain combines the two pictures sent to it by the two eyes and causes the person to "see" one picture with three dimensions.

3-D Movies

Have you ever seen a 3-D movie? In 3-D movies what is seen seems super-real. When watching a 3-D movie taken on a roller-coaster, the viewer feels as though he or she actually is on a roller-coaster, because the movie and the glasses worn while viewing combine to give depth to what is being seen. The principle used for 3-D movies is very similar to the one used for the stereopticon.

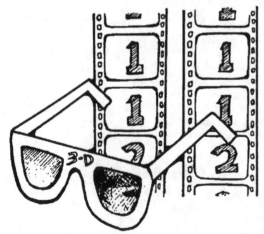

Two slightly different films are shown at the same time from two projectors placed side by side.

The two images are projected onto the same screen 2½ inches (6 cm) apart, the same distance apart as our eyes.

Looking through glasses, the viewer sees one image through the left lens and a slightly different image through the right lens. The brain puts the two images together.

3-D Glasses

In the 1950's, 3-D glasses were quite a fad. Wearing these special glasses to a 3-D movie or while viewing a comic book seemed to bring them to life! Although it is possible to purchase 3-D glasses in some novelty stores, you can easily make your own by following the directions on page 25. Create some 3-D pictures and enjoy the special effects by viewing them through the 3-D glasses.

3-D Vision *(cont.)*

Use the directions below to make your own 3-D glasses and pictures.

To Make 3-D Glasses:

1. Cut out the pattern parts at the bottom of the page. Trace the outline of the pattern parts onto tagboard. Color what you traced, then cut out the tagboard pieces.

2. Tape blue cellophane to the back of what will be the left lens and red cellophane to the back of what will be the right lens.

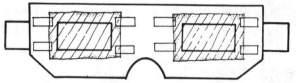

3. Fold the tabs on the main frame back. Tape the ear pieces to the main frame at the tabs after trimming any excess from the straight part first. (Be sure the curve of the ear piece faces down before you attach it to the main frame.)

How 3-D Glasses Work:

Using different colored lenses in front of your eyes causes momentary confusion in what you see because two different images of the same thing are being sent to your brain at the same time. The two different colored lenses do not actually produce 3-D vision—you already have that. They just confuse your brain so that it "flickers" back and forth between the two choices of data input, creating an illusion which, when you look at a two-dimensional picture, produces a "3-D" effect.

How to Create 3-D Pictures:

You will need red and light blue markers, pencils, or pens. On a sheet of paper, draw some red lines and some blue lines. How do they look through your 3-D glasses? Experiment with the red and blue lines to try to make 3-D geometric shapes, such as rectangular prisms, cones, or cylinders. Next, use the markers, pencils, or pens to create simple 3-D drawings. (Suggestions: A 3-D name, a person throwing a ball, a hand reaching out in your direction, a simple scene from *Dragonwings*.)

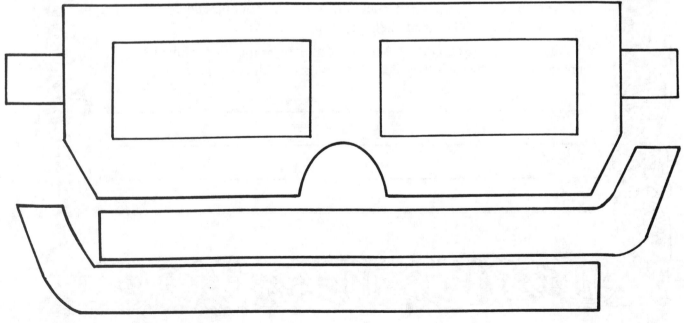

Promising Proverbs

Uncle Bright Star is continually using proverbs. A proverb is a short saying which expresses a well-known truth or fact about how people should live. Uncle's proverbs are all about his idea of "the superior man." He claims these sayings were first proclaimed by Confucius, a great Chinese philosopher who lived hundreds of years ago.

Some of Uncle's proverbs include:

Men must help one another in dangerous times and places.

Superior men help one another in time of need.

The superior man tends his own garden.

A superior man is above such things as getting wet.

A superior man shares his wealth in adversity.

Many proverbs have come down to us from the western world, too. How many of these have you heard before?

Nothing succeeds like success. (French)

Let the buyer beware. (Latin)

The way of a fool is right in his own eyes. (*The Bible*)

An apple a day keeps the doctor away. (Anonymous)

Activity

Find two proverbs to share with the class. Some helpful sources include *The Bible, Bartlett's Familiar Quotations, Poor Richard's Almanac* and sayings of famous people such as Shakespeare and Mark Twain. Your parents or grandparents may also be able to help you.

Write the two proverbs on the lines below. Think of examples or situations where these proverbs can be applied. Discuss them with your classmates.

_____

_____

_____

_____

Quiz Time

1. On the back of this page, name three important events in this section.

2. What is the Feast of Pure Brightness?

_____

_____

3. Describe what happens on April 18, 1906, thirteen days after the Feast of Pure Brightness.

_____

_____

4. How are most of the buildings in San Francisco destroyed?

_____

_____

5. Where do Moon Shadow, Windrider, Robin, and Miss Whitlaw go after the earthquake?

_____

_____

6. Why are the Tang people not allowed to stay where they had camped?

_____

_____

7. Who frequently speaks the words of Confucius?

_____

_____

8. How do many people act after the earthquake?

_____

_____

9. What happens to Jack?

_____

_____

10. Who supervises clean-up crews after the earthquake, and how?

_____

_____

Build a Model Seismograph

The first known mechanism to measure earthquakes was invented in China by the Chinese astronomer and mathematician, Chang Heng, in the year 132 A.D. This very interesting "earthquake weathercock" had eight dragons, each of which held a bronze ball in its mouth, all perching on the sides of a round seismoscope. A slight tremor would cause a ball to fall out of a dragon's mouth into the waiting mouth of a metal frog below. The direction of the first shaking was thought to be determined by which ball fell out. Chang Heng's seismoscope did not measure the intensity of the tremor, only its direction.

The first basic seismograph to measure the intensity of an earthquake was developed just before the beginning of the twentieth century. A photographic system was employed in this "seismometer." Light from a lamp shone through a hole in the tip of a pendulum. The pinpoint of light traced the seismic waves onto photographic paper.

Modern seismographs are very sensitive, but they still use the same basic pendulum principle of measurement used by the seismometer of 1899. Build a seismograph for the class to use. While it will not give you the exact picture of what the ground is doing during an earthquake, you will gain a greater understanding of just how a seismograph operates. Groups of students can work together to build a seismograph, or one can be made for the purposes of demonstration and testing by the entire class.

Directions

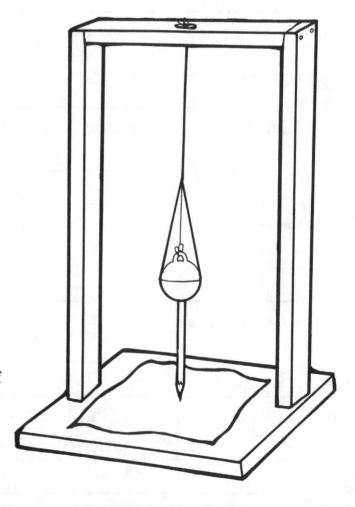

1. Construct a wooden frame, as shown, about 10 inches (25 cm) high by 5 inches (13 cm) wide.

2. In the exact center of the top wooden piece, drill a hole about $\frac{1}{16}$ inch (.2 cm) in diameter. Be sure an adult supervises this activity.

3. Suspend a piece of light fishing line through the hole, and secure it at the top of the frame.

4. Tie the lower end of the fishing line through the hole, and secure it at the top of the frame.

5. Tie the lower end of the fishing line to a number 1 deep sea fishing sinker, so it swings freely. Place a paper cone over the sinker as shown.

6. Into a small hole you have drilled in the bottom of the sinker, insert the ink cartridge of a ball point pen, so it hangs just touching a piece of paper. When a tremor hits, the pen will write onto the paper showing the tremor's movement.

Readers' Theater: "After the Quake"

The earthquake of 1906, while called "The San Francisco Earthquake," actually covered a very large area extending from Hollister to Fort Bragg, California, and more earthquake damage occurred in San Jose and Stanford than in San Francisco. However, Laurence Yep's account in *Dragonwings* of the events following the San Francisco Earthquake really did happen as he describes them, and the fire which followed the quake was what destroyed much of the city.

San Francisco in 1906 was a busy city of 400,000 people. Many of the buildings were wooden, and the "ham and eggs fire" was started by a woman trying to cook breakfast after the quake. The fire quickly spread across the city. Residents fled to Golden Gate Park, where a huge tent city was erected. Some people managed to crowd onto the ferries to cross over to Oakland or other parts of the northern bay area.

Discrimination against the Chinese had long been widespread in the city, and they had been denied education, harassed by the police, and exploited by the white business community. After the quake and before the fire, Chinatown was looted by National Guardsmen. The complaints of the Chinese Consul General that "the National Guard was stripping everything of value in Chinatown" were ignored by city officials, and looting was allowed to continue.

A powerful political figure in the city, Abe Reuf, called a meeting of the Subcommittee on Relocating the Chinese and told the business leaders who came that the Chinese "must not be allowed to return to the desirable area that Chinatown occupied." He had ulterior motives; he wanted to build a European development on the land. The subcommittee decided on Hunter Point, outside the city. However, because sending the Chinese to Hunter Point, which was in San Mateo County, would cause the loss of the taxes which the Chinese would pay, action was not taken on the plan. The subcommittee was unable to agree on another plan, and the Chinese, who owned a third of the land in Chinatown outright, began to return to rebuild.

Activity

In groups of three to five, write a scenario of an event which may have happened during or shortly after the earthquake. Each student in the group writes and performs a script in which he or she plays a character who tells about how the event affected the character and how the character saw it from his or her own perspective.

Some of the events which could be written about and performed might be witnessing a looting, taking the last ferry to Oakland to escape the fire, a meeting of the Subcommittee on Relocating the Chinese, a meeting of the Chinese leaders to discuss returning to Chinatown, watching a tenement building collapse and trying to save the people in it, or camping in Golden Gate Park. You may choose a different event, if you wish. After practicing together, read your scenario to the class as a group.

Fly a Paper Airplane

Directions: Listen to directions given by your teacher. You will be making a paper airplane. The object is to design one that will perform the best that it can. Consider adjustments in the shape, measurements, weight, etc., as you work on your paper airplane. When you are done, have a paper airplane flying contest.

Activity

Before making your airplane, measure and record the following:

Length of paper _____

Width of paper _____

Area of paper _____

Perimeter of paper _____

After making your airplane, measure and record the following:

Length of plane _____

Width of wingspan _____

Width of tail _____

Depth of fuselage (body) _____

Now fly all the airplanes. Which one flew the farthest? _____

After watching all the planes fly and seeing which of them did best, can you determine which type of plane flew best and which type flew the longest distance? Write your observations here.

_____

_____

_____

_____

_____

_____

_____

_____

Lost Kitten

Whenever natural disasters occur, there are many small victims, such as family pets. Imagine that you were present during the San Francisco Earthquake. You have found a small gray kitten wandering through the ruins looking for its owners. You know you are unable to keep the kitten, and you are certain someone is missing it very badly.

In the space below, design a poster to distribute in the area where you found the kitten. Include information that will inform the owner that his kitten is safe and where it can be claimed.

Quiz Time

1. On the back of this paper, name three important events from this section.

2. Where is Moon Shadow and Windrider's new home?

    _____

3. How does Moon Shadow's mother react to the story that Windrider was once physician to the Dragon King?

    _____

    _____

4. Moon Shadow says, "All about me, I had Father's dream taking visible form." To what is he referring?

    _____

    _____

    _____

5. Describe Dragonwings.

    _____

    _____

6. Why does Moon Shadow have the feeling that someone or something has been into where he and his father lived?

    _____

    _____

7. How is Dragonwings christened?

    _____

    _____

8. Who does Moon Shadow find in the barn, and what is he doing?

    _____

    _____

9. How did Father become a partner and a merchant?

    _____

    _____

10. On the back of this paper, tell the story of the first flight of Dragonwings. Include what happened, who was there, and how the flight ended.

Be a Designer

Windrider is more than just an important figure in Moon Shadow's life; Windrider is Moon Shadow's hero, his idol. He is everything that Moon Shadow would want to be, and Moon Shadow will do anything for his father.

Laurence Yep gives the reader two symbols for Windrider: a flying machine and some of his kites, which also are very imaginative and in many shapes and colors.

In the early days of aviation, many different types of flying machines were built. Some had two or more wings. Many used the principle of a bird in flight, even attempting to build wings to attach to a person's arms. Others took the form of kites or of huge hot air balloons. Hot air balloons and blimps, today's dirigibles, are still in use. More than once, kites were used to carry soldiers high into the air to enable them to observe the enemy's movement. Of course, a few soldiers were lost that way, because they made easy targets!

Use your imagination to design either a kite or a flying machine. Consider what you are going to design. Will it be a kite? If so, what shape will it take? A bird? An insect? A geometric shape?

Or will your design be of a flying machine? Again, what shape will it take? Will it be an aeroplane with two, or three, or more wings? Will it be like a flying cigar, as some early ones were? Will it carry one person or more?

You might even decide to draw your own idea of Dragonwings. You're only limited by how far you will let your imagination soar!

Go to the library, and look at pictures of the early flying machines and kites. Read about the many different ideas that early designers had. They may give you ideas of your own.

Begin by drawing a rough sketch and refine it as you proceed. Take time, and really think about your design. As you begin to get closer to your final design, it might help to use graph paper to give your creation a better perspective.

Your final design of a flying machine may be a picture, or it can be a model. Or you may choose to build a kite. Whichever you choose to do, use your creative ability to make the design truly yours.

Aviation Trivia

Working in a group of three or four students, research to locate the information below. You may not be able to find all of the answers—try your best to find as many as possible. When your group has finished, share your findings with the other groups. Include a discussion of any other interesting aviation facts you may have discovered as you did your research.

1. The first successful hot air balloonist

   _____

2. The first manned supersonic airplane

   _____

3. First woman to fly faster than the speed of sound

   _____

4. Mythological man whose wings melted when he got too close to the sun

   _____

5. American brothers who made the first manned, controlled flight

   _____

6. Name of the first plane to cross the Atlantic Ocean

   _____

7. Pilot of the first plane to cross the Atlantic Ocean

   _____

8. The first wide-bodied airliner

   _____

9. The world's largest passenger jet plane

   _____

10. Howard Hughes' huge plane which flew only once

    _____

11. American woman lost at sea in an attempt to fly around the world

    _____

12. First in-flight refueling

    _____

13. First known parachute designer

    _____

14. First helicopter designed for military service

    _____

15. First human to set foot on the moon

    _____

Up, Up, and Away

Have you ever wondered how an airplane gets up into the air and flies? An airplane is very much like a bird. The plane's wing is an *airfoil*, curved on top and almost flat on the bottom. Thrust is the force that pulls a plane forward by allowing air to flow above and below the wings. In planes that use propellers to create thrust, the propeller serves to move as much air by as possible in order to create the greatest forward movement. In a jet plane, the jet engine replaces the propeller in moving air to create thrust.

When air flows back over the top and bottom of the wing, the shape of the airfoil causes the air flowing over the top of the wing to travel farther than the air flowing under the wing. This air going over the top has to go faster to catch up with the air going under the wing.

When this happens, the faster moving air on top has less pressure than the air pressure under the wing. The greater pressure under the wing causes the wing to "lift," and the wing is pushed up.

The pilot steers the plane with a steering column and two pedals which move a rudder on the tail of the plane. A control column drives the *elevators* that run across the tail of the plane. The pilot pulls back on the control column to make the plane climb, and pushes forward on it to drop. Ailerons are the flaps on the edges of the wings which move up and down, changing the shape of the wings and the way the air flow strikes the wings. The pilot uses these to turn right or left and to perform other maneuvers. The body of the plane is called the *fuselage*.

Study the sketches below. When you feel that you are ready to identify the parts, label the blank lines on page 36 with the correct parts.

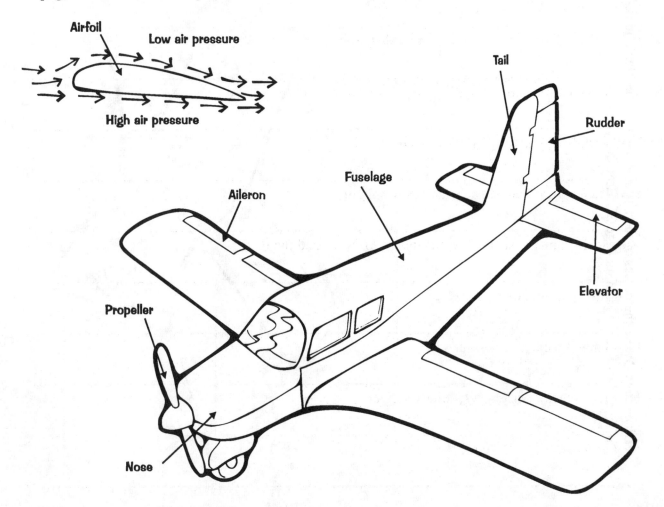

Up, Up, and Away *(cont.)*

Directions: Write the names of the airplane parts on the blank lines. When you are finished, compare your answers with the labelled diagram on page 35. How did you do?

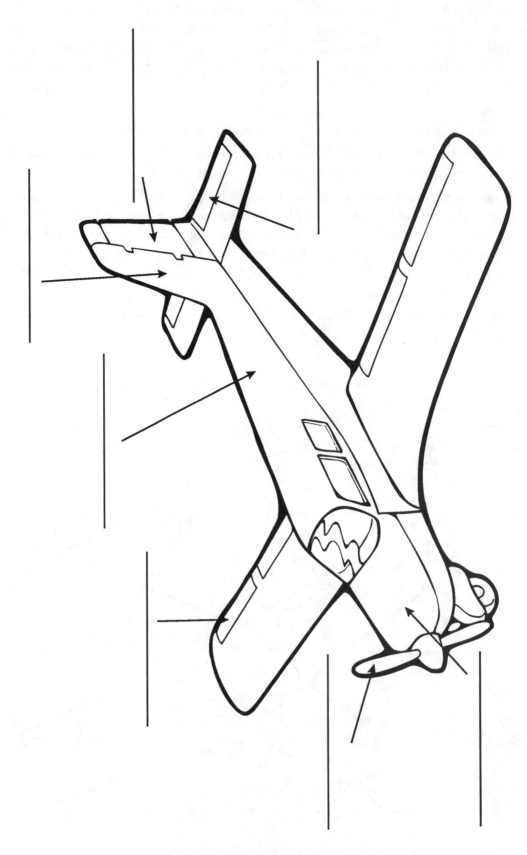

Letter to Mother

By the time Windrider is ready to bring Moon Shadow's mother to San Francisco, Moon Shadow has not seen her for several years. He's grown from being a very young boy to being a young man. Many important events have taken place, and many changes have occurred.

Imagine that you are Moon Shadow. Write a letter to your mother telling her what to expect when she arrives. How will life be different here than it is in the Middle Kingdom? How will you have changed? How will your father have changed after the twelve years of separation from her? (Remember to tell her how happy you are that she will finally be joining you and your father!)

_____ ,

Reading Response Journal Questions

See page 15 for directions on how to use the following chapter questions.

Chapter 1
- Describe Grandmother's idea of the Land of the Golden Mountain.

Chapter 2
- Describe the town of the Tang people. What is its present name?
- How did Moon Shadow's father and the people of the Tang welcome him when he came?
- Who was Black Dog and what did he announce was going to happen?

Chapter 3
- How did Windrider get his name?
- Who was the Dragon King?
- Describe the dragon's kingdom.

Chapter 4
- Who were the "Old Ones"?
- How did Moon Shadow and Windrider meet the demon, Mr. Alger?
- What is it that fascinates Windrider so much? Why?

Chapter 5
- How did Black Dog explain away his terrible habit?
- What happened between Father and Black Dog, and what was the end result of it?

Chapter 6
- Describe Moon Shadow and Windrider's new home.
- Why was Moon Shadow reluctant to drink milk and eat gingerbread cookies?
- What are some differences between the dragons the demoness knew about and the dragons Moon Shadow knew about?

Chapter 7
- How did Moon Shadow educate Miss Whitlaw?
- How did Robin teach Moon Shadow to read English?
- To whom did Moon Shadow write, and what was the end result of it?

Chapter 8
- What special thing did Moon Shadow, Windrider, and Robin do on their picnic?
- What secret did Robin tell Moon Shadow about Jack, and how did it help him?

Chapter 9
- Describe the earthquake as Moon Shadow felt and saw it.
- How did Miss Whitlaw get people to help following the earthquake?
- What response did the people of the Tang have to Miss Whitlaw, and what did Windrider call her?

Chapter 10
- What is the meaning of this proverb of Uncle's: "The superior man shares his wealth in adversity?"
- To where did the people of the Tang move, and why?

Chapter 11
- How did Moon Shadow's mother respond to the information that her husband had been physician to the Dragon King?
- Describe Dragonwings.

Chapter 12
- Who came to see Dragonwings fly?
- How did Father pay the rent?
- Describe the flight of Dragonwings.

Book Report Ideas

After finishing a good book, there are many ways to report on it. The possibilities are as endless as your imagination! Here are some suggestions of ways you might choose to report on *Dragonwings*, or you may come up with one of your own.

- **Write a letter to the author.** The author may not have time to respond to your letter. But authors like to receive letters from their readers, and they especially enjoy hearing from young people who have read their books, because it gives them feedback from a young person's point of view. Be sure to enclose a stamped, self-addressed envelope just in case the author does have time to answer your letter. Send the letter in care of the novel's publisher.

- **Write a character sketch** of a character in *Dragonwings*. When doing this, remember the main ways of describing a person: describe the way he or she looks; describe the things he or she does and how he or she does them; describe the way others react to him or her. Don't forget to include some of of the things the character says.

- **Draw an early plane** to scale to illustrate how Windrider's plane may have looked. The dimensions are given to you in *Dragonwings*. Do some research in the library to see how it may have looked.

- **Give a demonstration** of how a seismograph works or what it shows about an earthquake. The people in 1906 did not have the kinds of modern equipment which modern science has, but if you check with a branch of the U.S. Geological Survey or with a major university such as the University of California, you can get a great deal of information to help you show your classmates just how horrendous was the 1906 San Francisco earthquake which Moon Shadow describes in *Dragonwings*.

- **Create a billboard advertising the book** *Dragonwings*. Use posterboard and draw the wooden frame on with brown markers.

- **Write a story of aviation.** It may seem strange to believe, but people have flown in airplanes less than a hundred years. Nevertheless, stories of man and flight have been around at least since Icarus tried to fly in Ancient Greece, and Leonardo da Vinci drew plans for a helicopter hundreds of years ago.

- **Make a soap carving** of a character or animal from Chinese history or mythology. Carvings of stone, wood, and even of glass have been made by the Chinese for thousands of years.

- **Make a mobile** of models of early airplanes or helicopters. Remember how Windrider had models hanging from the ceiling of the barn? Make your own!

- **Create "This Is Your Life, Windrider."** One person role plays the character, and an announcer describes important people and events in the life of the character being honored.

- **Interview a character in** *Dragonwings*.

- **Write an episode from Robin's point of view.** The episode might be the one in which Moon Shadow meets Robin for the first time, or her impression of him when he drank his first milk and ate his first gingerbread cookie.

Research Ideas

Describe three things that you read in *Dragonwings* that you would like to learn more about.

1. _____

2. _____

3. _____

In *Dragonwings*, you encountered many real people and events, customs, lifestyles, inventions, history, religious beliefs, and ways of looking at the world which may be much different than those you have known before. Learning some background information will help you to understand the book much better, as well as be more aware of Laurence Yep's tremendous ability to write a wonderful story.

Work in groups or alone to research at least one of the areas you named above or the areas that are listed below. Share what you learn with the rest of the class in an oral presentation.

- History of aviation
- Wilbur and Orville Wright
- Chinese dynasties
- Manchus
- Theodore Roosevelt
- History of San Francisco
- Angel Island
- Chinese mythology
- Dragons
- Chinese proverbs
- Chinese New Year
- Chinese holidays
- The San Francisco Fire
- Golden Gate Park
- Martial law
- Buddhism
- Airplane mechanics
- Dime novels
- Victorian houses
- Magic lantern shows
- Shakers
- Boarding houses
- Gliders
- Ned Buntline
- Crystal sets
- Confucius

- Early airplanes
- The San Francisco Earthquake
- Kite making
- Seismographs
- History of China
- Chinese calligraphy
- Chinese immigration
- Earthquakes
- Building an airplane
- The Opium Wars
- Chinese calendar
- Chinese cooking
- Chinatown
- Stereopticons
- *The Highwayman*
- The Presidio
- Designing an airplane
- Gas lamps
- Horseless carriages
- Stained glass windows
- St. George and the dragon
- Water pumps
- Abacus
- Buffalo Bill
- Electric lights
- Dirigibles

Chinese Festival

Do you remember the picnic that Moon Shadow, Windrider, Robin, and Miss Whitlaw had? What a time they all had at the beach, eating good food and flying the glider! Many people like Chinese food, and most cities have any number of Chinese restaurants. What better way to celebrate the finishing of *Dragonwings* than with a meal of favorite Chinese foods and a kite festival such as the boys and girls in China have every year!

Most of the work of a festival lies in the preparation, so let's get started! When planning an activity for the entire class, it usually is best to divide responsibilities so that everyone has a chance to participate. The following are some of the committees you may wish to form and the jobs that each can undertake:

- **Site Committee:** Decide where the luncheon will be held. Will you invite others? Will you need invitations?

- **Decoration Committee:** Design and make decorations for the room or outdoor area where the luncheon will be held. Will you use the Chinese lanterns you made earlier?

- **Table Preparations:** Design place mats and table decorations. Do you want a color scheme? Red, green, and yellow are good choices.

- **Rules Committee:** Draw up a list of rules for the kite festival and contest. Will you have separate rules for gliders and kites? Will you judge them strictly on beauty, or on how well they fly?

- **Clean-up Committee:** Everyone's favorite! Guess what the members of this committee will do.

Food

There are several ways to go about getting the food. One way would be to have the food brought in. Most Chinese restaurants have a take-out service, so if the class members wish to check into having food brought in, and if everyone is agreeable to each paying a certain amount, this may be preferable. Some schools will have a fund, such as a student body fund or one established by the parents' organization, which might finance at least part of the amount needed. If your school has an on-grounds cafeteria, you may be able to work something out with them in terms of using the school facilities or helping with the preparation. Another alternative to providing the food could be to select a Foods Committee to prepare all or some of the food.

Chinese Festival *(cont.)*

Chinese food is fairly simple to prepare, with very small amounts of meat and lots of rice and vegetables. Many large supermarkets now have prepared Chinese foods, some of them frozen and ready to pop into a microwave or an oven. If you plan to prepare a dish "from scratch," try one or both of the recipes on this page.

However you get the food to the festival site, you need to plan a menu first. Some suggestions might be fried rice, chow mein, egg rolls, lemon chicken, or chicken wings. Don't forget the fortune cookies and tea!

Recipes

Marbled Eggs

Ingredients:

- 6 hard-boiled eggs
- 1 tablespoon (15 mL) soy sauce
- 1 teaspoon (5 mL) dry ginger

- 2 tablespoons (30 mL) brown sugar
- 1/2 teaspoon (3 mL) Chinese five-spice
- 1 cinnamon stick

Directions: Gently tap the shell of each egg with a spoon until small cracks appear over the entire egg. Bring the remaining ingredients to a boil. Reduce heat to simmer, and cook about 15 minutes. Place the eggs in the sauce mixture and cook them very slowly for 1 hour. If needed, add water to cover the eggs. After one hour, turn off the heat and let the eggs cool in liquid. Refrigerate the marbled eggs overnight. Just before serving, peel off the eggshells carefully and serve.

Chicken Wings

Ingredients

- 6 chicken wings
- 1 green onion, chopped
- 1/2 cup (125 mL) soy sauce
- 1 tablespoon (15 mL) brown sugar
- 1 tablespoon (15 mL) dry ginger

- 1 cinnamon stick
- 2 teaspoons (10 mL) cooking oil
- 2 1/2 teaspoons (13 mL) cornstarch
- 2 tablespoons (30 mL) water
- 1 cup (250 mL) chicken broth

Directions: Soak the wings in soy sauce for 2 hours. Quickly cook the wings in hot oil over medium heat until they are lightly browned. Mix the chicken broth, soy sauce, brown sugar, green onion, and ginger in a sauce pan, and bring it to a boil. Lower the heat. Add the wings to the sauce and simmer about 15 minutes until wings are tender.

In a separate sauce pan, thicken 1/2 cup (125 mL) of the sauce with cornstarch which has been stirred into cold water, and pour the mixture over the wings. Serve.

Kite and Glider Festival

Many Chinese boys and girls participate in kite contests each year. For the festival, fly homemade kites or have students bring in pre-made kites, gliders, or model planes. Directions for making your own kites are provided on page 17. Fill the sky with your colorful and creative kites and gliders. What a wonderful way to spend an afternoon!

Objective Test and Essay

Matching: Match the descriptions of the characters with their names.

_____	1. Hand Clap	a. tells frightening stories about demons
_____	2. Black Dog	b. wants to be a superior man
_____	3. Grandfather	c. makes wonderful gingerbread cookies
_____	4. Jack	d. takes his time going up the hill
_____	5. Grandmother	e. was a good man but is not anymore
_____	6. Robin	f. was lynched as soon as he reached California
_____	7. Windrider	g. physician to the Dragon King
_____	8. Uncle Bright Star	h. tells tall tales
_____	9. Moon Shadow	i. got a well-deserved bloody nose
_____	10. Mr. Alger	j. reads dime novels
_____	11. Miss Whitlaw	k. teaches the demoness about dragons
_____	12. Red Rabbit	l. a good demon who hires Windrider

True or False: Answer true or false in the blanks below.

_____ 1. Black Dog helped Moon Shadow when he was attacked by the demons.

_____ 2. The people of the Tang thought Windrider was crazy but still supported him in his venture.

_____ 3. Moon Shadow and Robin had the same opinion about milk.

_____ 4. The Wright brothers were jealous of Windrider's work and would not help him.

_____ 5. When Windrider's flying machine crashed, he immediately began to build another.

Short Answer: On separate paper, write a brief answer to each question below.

1. Besides Moon Shadow and Windrider, name three people of the Tang.
2. What do the demons of San Francisco think of the people of the Tang?
3. Where is the Middle Kingdom?
4. How did Windrider get his name?
5. What terrible event happened to San Francisco, and how did the people react to it?

Essay: On the back of this paper, respond to the following.

To the people of the Tang and to Miss Whitlaw and Robin, helping each other is very important in everyday life. During the earthquake, however, some San Franciscans were reluctant to help others and were only out for themselves. Describe the differences between the way in which Miss Whitlaw and the Tang people reacted after the earthquake and the way in which some others behaved. Then tell whether you think Miss Whitlaw was right, and why you think so.

Essay Challenge: Include in your essay some specific ways in which one might help during a disaster.

Response

Explain the meaning of these quotations from *Dragonwings*.

Chapter 1   *I thought to myself, How can we ever speak to one another? He's as strange to me as the demon.*

Chapter 2   *Which one is the Golden Mountain?*

Chapter 2   *'Welcome to the land of the demons, boy,' Black Dog laughed grimly.*

Chapter 3   *Every other inch of space in the room was crowded with small, strangely constructed machines whose purpose I could not guess.*

Chapter 3   *The object that he had treated so casually was beautifully meticulous. It was a work of art.*

Chapter 4   *Because a demon can help or harm you, there is no way of telling if a demon might be testing you before he will reward you or whether he is trying to trick you.*

Chapter 4   *'Remember,' Father said, 'he was a good man once. Now go get his things.'*

Chapter 5   *Ten days later, the poor farmer noticed a strange white flower growing from her grave.*

Chapter 5   *Then I realized that to be a dragon meant more than just taking an interest in the magic of machines. It was also to live by the spirit of dragons.*

Chapter 6   *It seemed to me at that time that there might be any number of demons waiting in their houses, waiting patiently for me to turn my back so they could leap upon me and take over my body, or torture me, or do the hundred and one things that demons can do to people.*

Chapter 6   *'It's a very wicked animal that breathes fire and goes about eating up people and destroying towns. St. George killed many of them.'*

Chapter 7   *I felt a vague sense of triumph at having made them use their biggest weapons.*

Chapter 7   *She slipped some dime novels from behind her back. They were printed on cheap tan-colored paper with the most lurid paper covers, and they ranged across a wide variety of subjects.*

Chapter 8   *For one moment, he watched, satisfied, as the glider tugged at the string in his hand and the poem fluttered. Then, with a sudden sweep, he cut the cord.*

Chapter 9   *It seemed like a nightmare where everything you take to be rock-hard, solid brass for reality becomes unreal.*

Chapter 9   *It was not until months later that we learned how it started.*

Chapter 10 *One day we were living in a law abiding community and the next day the city and the community had both dissolved, with every person for himself.*

Chapter 10 *'The superior man shares his wealth in adversity.'*

Chapter 11 *'There,' he said, stepping back. 'If we can't chase out the smell, maybe we can cover it up.'*

Chapter 11 *Mother was patient and understanding, saying what a truly wonderful thing it was to meet the Dragon King.*

Chapter 12 *Toiling up the hill out of the fog was Red Rabbit, and behind him I saw Uncle on the wagon seat.*

Conversations

Working in size-appropriate groups, write and perform the conversation which might have occurred in one of the following situations. You may use an idea of your own for a conversation between characters in *Dragonwings*.

- Moon Shadow describes to his mother and grandmother the flight of Dragonwings. *(3 people)*

- Moon Shadow and Robin discuss which drink is better for one's health: jasmine tea or milk. *(2 people)*

- Miss Whitlaw and mother compare the life of women in the China of 1910 and San Francisco of the same time. *(2 people)*

- Windrider and the Wright brothers actually meet and combine their designs to make a new and better aeroplane. *(3 people)*

- Black Dog gives up opium and apologizes to Moon Shadow. *(2 people)*

- Windrider tells Moon Shadow's son about Dragonwings. *(2 people)*

- Moon Shadow teaches Robin how to write Chinese characters. *(2 people)*

- Robin explains to Miss Whitlaw where she found the dime novels. *(2 people)*

- Miss Whitlaw presents Windrider to the mayor of Oakland and describes the flight of Dragonwings. *(3 people)*

- The doctor talks to Windrider about going up in flying machines. *(2 people)*

- Moon Shadow explains his father's accomplishment to the Dragon King. *(2 people)*

- Uncle tells Robin's son how to be a superior man. *(2 people)*

- The President of the United States presents an honorary award to Windrider for having conquered the air. *(2 people)*

- Moon Shadow, Windrider, Robin, and Miss Whitlaw celebrate Chinese New Year together in 1920. *(4 people)*

- Moon Shadow describes to Robin's little boy the swallow kite he has just made for him. *(2 people)*

- Moon Shadow tells Robin about his stay on Angel Island. *(2 people)*

Bibliography

Crafts and Resource Books

Bolt, Bruce *A. Earthquakes, A Primer.* (W.H. Freeman and Company, 1978)

Bresnick, Perry. *Leaving for America.* (Children's Book Press, 1992)

Consumer Guide. *The Big Book of How Things Work.* (Publications International Limited, 1991)

The Danbury Press. *The Illustrated Encyclopedia of the Animal Kingdom.* (Grolier Enterprises, Inc., 1972)

Entwistle, Theodore Rowland. *Confucius & Ancient China.* (Bookwright Press, 1987)

Freedman, Russell. *Immigrant Kids.* (Scholastic, 1992)

Gere, James M. and Haresh C. *Shah. Terra Non Firma.* (W.H. Freeman and Company, 1984)

Greene, Amsel. *Pullet Surprises.* (Scott, Foresman and Company, 1969)

Handforth, Thomas. *Mei Li China.* (Doubleday, 1955)

Harris, Sherwood. *The First to Fly.* (Simon and Schuster, 1970)

Houston, Jeanne Wakatsuki. *Farewell to Manzanar.* (Bantam Books Inc., 1974)

Iacopi, Robert. *Earthquake Country.* (Lane Publishing Co., 1981)

Kohn, Bernice. *The Organic Living Book.* (The Viking Press, 1972)

Lambert, David. *Earthquakes and Volcanoes.* (The Bookwright Press, 1986)

Mondey, David, Editor. *An Illustrated History of Aircraft.* (Quarto Publishing, Ltd., 1980)

Mondey, David, and Michael J.H. Taylor. *The Guinness Book of Aircraft* (Guinness, 1988)

Overholt, Dr. James L. *Dr. Jim's Elementary Math Prescriptions.* (Goodyear Publishing Company, Inc., 1978)

Philbrick, Helen and John. *The Bug Book.* (Storey Communications, Inc., 1974)

Rombauer, Irma S. and Marion Rombauer Becker. *The Joy of Cooking.* (The Bobbs-Merrill Company, Inc., 1953)

Rosenbloom, Joseph. *Daffy Definitions.* (Wings Books, 1977)

Ross, Frank Jr. *Historic Plane Models.* (Lothrop, Lee, and Shepard, Co., 1973)

Sandin, Joan. *The Long Way to a New Land.* (Harper & Row, 1981)

Smith, Robert T. *Building and Flying Rubber Band-Powered Airplanes.* (Tab Books, Inc., 1982)

Thomas, Gordon, and Max Morgan Witts. *The San Francisco Earthquake.* (Stein and Day, 1971)

Walker, Bryce, and the Editors of Time-Life Books. *Earthquake.* (Time-Life Books, 1982)

Warner, Bill. *Building the Sky Bunny.* (Tab Books, Inc., 1992)

Wartski, Maureen Crane. *A Boat to Nowhere* (Westminster/John Knox Press, 1980)

Weiss, Harvey. *Model Airplanes and How to Build Them.* (Thomas Y. Crowell Company, 1975)

Yep, Laurence. *Child of the Owl.* (Harper Trophy, 1977)

Answer Key

Page 10
1. Hand Clap says it.
2. The Chinese people call themselves People of the Tang.
3. They are taken to the barracks at Angel Island.
4. Accept all appropriate responses.
5. He was lynched when he first came to San Francisco.
6. A demon can be the ghost of a dead person, a supernatural creature, a white person, or an "American devil."
7. They work by doing laundry.
8. The Chinese men are not allowed to bring wives or children unless the man is a merchant.
9. Uncle Bright Star takes his ideas from Confucius.
10. The "silly toy" is a butterfly-shaped kite made from bamboo sticks and brightly-colored rice paper.

Page 16
1. Accept appropriate responses.
2. Black Dog causes problems.
3. Black Dog steals the money Moon Shadow had collected for the laundry.
4. It is very expensive, and men are discouraged from bringing their wives because it is also dangerous.
5. Mr. Alger's horseless carriage breaks down. Windrider is able to fix it on the spot, so Mr. Alger offers him work.
6. He has a dream in which he believes to have actually visited the Dragon King, and the Dragon King tells him he had been a dragon in another life.
7. Accept any appropriate answers.
8. He will take jobs fixing machines for the demons.
9. He has a natural talent for knowing how to fix anything mechanical.
10. Accept appropriate responses.

Page 21
1. Accept appropriate answers.
2. Moon Shadow calls Miss Whitlaw the "demoness."

3. Windrider is horrified and calls Moon Shadow a pig; Miss Whitlaw is delighted and feels it is a compliment.
4. Moon Shadow thinks dragons are mostly good, although sometimes bad. Miss Whitlaw thinks they are terrible creatures.
5. Robin tells Moon Shadow that Jack cannot stand being hit in the nose, so Moon Shadow deliberately antagonizes Jack, then bloodies his nose.
6. Robin uses dime novels, E. Nesbit books, and Ned Buntline.
7. Moon Shadow writes a letter to the Wright brothers. Orville Wright answers him, and they begin a correspondence about flying.
8. They go to the beach, and after eating they fly Windrider's glider. After flying the glider, Windrider cuts the cord and lets the glider go.
9. Moon Shadow educates Miss Whitlaw about dragons and Chinese tea. Miss Whitlaw educates Moon Shadow about American ways.
10. Windrider wants to build a flying machine and fly it more than anything. He swallows his pride and studies all the Wright brothers' letters as to how to build it.

Page 27
1. Accept appropriate answers.
2. It is a feast honoring the dead in which the Tang people go to the cemetery with food for the dead, then go home and eat.
3. This is the date of the San Francisco earthquake.
4. Most of the buildings are destroyed by fire.
5. They go to Golden Gate Park.
6. All the Chinese are forced to leave Golden Gate Park for racial reasons.
7. Uncle Bright Star frequently refers to the words of Confucius.
8. Accept appropriate answers.
9. He is killed when the tenement he lives in collapses.
10. Miss Whitlaw organizes people and directs (sometimes forcefully) them in cleaning-up efforts.

Page 30

Teacher Directions: Fly a Paper Airplane

This activity can be done using either the metric system or the English system of measurements. The only materials needed are assorted sheets of paper, pencils, and measuring sticks using either centimeters or inches.

First, discuss with the students what might make a paper airplane fly. Explain that some will fly better than others, but in this assignment, they will design and fly their own. They will take various measurements, so discuss the different measurements they are going to take: length, width, area, perimeter, depth, etc.

Distribute sheets of paper in varying sizes, the measuring sticks, and copies of the activity on page 30.

Page 32

1. Accept appropriate answers.
2. Their new home is on the outskirts of Oakland.
3. She writes to Moon Shadow telling him she had had no idea that it had been true, but that she is very proud.
4. All around him are models, gliders, and a flying machine which Windrider has been building.
5. Accept appropriate responses which agree with description in this book.
6. Black Dog has been looking for money there.

7. Miss Whitlaw and Robin come and they have a little celebration, christening Dragonwings with a small bottle of wine.
8. He finds Black Dog looking for money.
9. Uncle Bright Star loaned him $1,000 with no interest and the company invited him to join as a partner.
10. Accept appropriate answers.

Page 34

1. Francoise Pilatre de Rozier, 1783
2. American Bell X-1 flown by Charles "Chuck" Yeager, 1946
3. Jaqueline Cochran, 1953
4. Icarus
5. Wright Brothers, 1903
6. The "Spirit of Saint Louis"
7. Charles Lindberg
8. Boeing 747
9. The Concorde
10. The "Spruce Goose"
11. Amelia Earhart
12. KB-29 tankers to F-84E Thunderjets, May 29, 1952
13. Leonardo da Vinci
14. Sikorski XR-4, January 13, 1942
15. Neil Armstrong, July 21, 1969

Page 43

Matching

1. h	7. g
2. e	8. b
3. f	9. k
4. i	10. l
5. a	11. c
6. j	12. d

True-False

1. F
2. T
3. F
4. F
5. F

Short Answer

1. Include any three of the following: Uncle Bright Star, Hand Clap, Tiger General, White Deer, Black Dog, any Chinese people named in the story.
2. Many of the white people of San Francisco are prejudiced against the Chinese. They do not like them because they will take any jobs they can get, because they eat differently than Americans, and for many other reasons.
3. The Middle Kingdom is the Chinese name for China.
4. Windrider got his name from the Dragon King.
5. The earthquake of 1906. Accept appropriate responses.

Essay and Essay Challenge

Accept well supported responses, reactions, and opinions.